The Enigma Plot

Written by Roderick Hunt
and illustrated by Alex Brychta

OXFORD
UNIVERSITY PRESS

Before reading

- Read the back cover text and page 4. Why might the Virans be interested in the Second World War?
- Look at page 4. Why do you think people had to send secret messages in code?

After reading

- How different was life for the evacuees compared to children today?

Book quiz

1 What was 'Enigma' used for?
  a Sending evacuees to the countryside.
  b Sending secret messages.
  c Covering people's windows during a blackout.
2 What is odd about the woman's name?
3 What were evacuees?

See p44 for the book quiz answers!

Before you begin ...

Biff, Chip, Kipper and friends have become Time Runners. They are based in the Time Vault, which exists outside time. Their mission is to travel back in time to defeat the Virans, who are trying to destroy history and bring chaos to the future.

The Time Runners have a Zaptrap - a device to capture the Virans - and a Link, which lets them communicate with the Time Vault. Apart from that, they are on their own!

The Enigma Machine, 1941

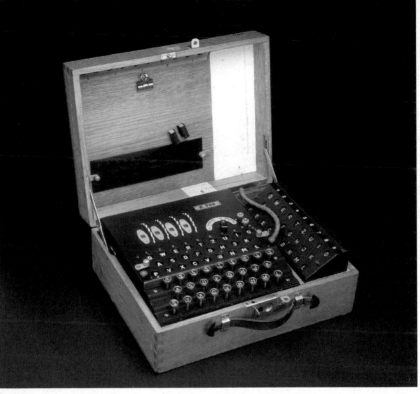

During World War 2 the Nazis sent secret messages using machines called 'Enigma'. The message was typed on the machine's keyboard. Every time a key was pressed, the Enigma machine changed that letter. Messages became totally scrambled and almost impossible to decode. Unless, that is, the person who received the message also had an Enigma machine and knew the settings. If only Britain could crack the Enigma code!

Chapter 1

The Major stared at the papers on his desk and gasped. Then he spoke to the woman sitting in front of him.

"You scored 96% in our test. It's the highest score I have ever seen."

The woman's eyes met his. They were so cold and piercing, they made the Major shudder.

The woman gave an icy smile. "Yes," she said. "I like working out puzzles and I enjoy solving codes."

The Major gulped. His eyes were locked in the woman's stare. He felt a coldness creep up his body.

"I see you speak fluent German and Russian," he said.

The woman spoke softly. "I speak many other languages."

She stared coldly at the Major.

"Well, er, Miss Vinar," he went on. "You can begin at once. The work is a vital part of the war effort." The Major found it hard to speak properly. "It is, and must be, absolutely secret. Abso ... er ... secret ... lutely."

He picked up a paper. The woman gently pulled it from his hand. "Ah! The Official Secrets Act," she said.

As she signed the paper, her eyes did not leave the Major's. "You will find I am very good at my work," she said.

"Can't ... think ... cold ... so ... why ... I ... am?" the Major gasped.

"Oh, I can," hissed Miss Vinar.

Chapter 2

Neena was beating Wilf at computer tennis when the alarm went off in the Time Vault. Tyler was pressing the alarm button, on ... off ... on ... off! The call was urgent.

"It's a tricky one," Tyler said when everyone was in the control room. "I can't quite make it out."

A dark spot had appeared on the TimeWeb like a black hole.

"It looks as if the Virans are on to something big," said Neena.

"It's high up on the web," said Kipper, "so it can't be that long ago."

Tyler keyed the Matrix. Then he peered at the globe that glowed beside it. "Somewhere in England in 1941," he said. "Look, it's a big house near a railway line. I don't get it."

"Well, 1941 was near the beginning of World War Two," said Biff. "So what are the Virans up to?"

"Who's going on this one?" asked Chip.

"I think Wilma," urged Neena. "But let her choose who goes with her."

Tyler tapped the portal key on the Matrix, and at once, a doorway appeared next to the TimeWeb. Wilma, Nadim and Kipper stepped into it. "Good luck," called Wilf as Tyler tapped the 'send' key on the Matrix.

Chapter 3

The three of them arrived together.
They were in a corridor that smelled of polish, disinfectant and sour milk.

From behind a door they could hear children chanting.

"Four nines are thirty six. Five nines are forty five ..."

"It's a school," said Wilma. "These are classroom doors."

Suddenly, a bell rang and children began to rush out of the classrooms. It was home time.

"Don't run!" shouted a man's voice.

One boy lagged behind. As he ran out, a girl tripped him up. A few children began to chant, "Evacuees, dirty knees. You've got nits and lice and fleas."

"We've got to stop this," said Wilma. "Come on!" She ran to the group of children. "Leave him alone," she yelled.

The children looked surprised.

"Who are you?" one asked. "We ain't never seen you before."

"Never mind who we are," said Wilma. "Clear off! You're just a load of bullies."

The children ran off. As Kipper pulled the boy to his feet, he saw he had been crying.

The boy told them that he had been evacuated in June 1940 with all the children at his school.

"It's safer in the country, in case of bombs. But I miss my Mum. She's still in London. I worry about her."

DOWNLOAD FROM TYLER

In World War II, kids living in big towns went to live in the country. In 1940 100,000 were evacuated! Imagine it!

"I was evacuated to Bedford," the boy
went on, "but the people I live with, Mr and
Mrs King, moved to Bletchley. They both got
jobs here so I came with them. I'm the only
evacuee in the school."

Nadim took his Link from his pocket.
They needed help from Tyler back in the
Time Vault. "Tyler," he whispered. "Why are
we in a school?"

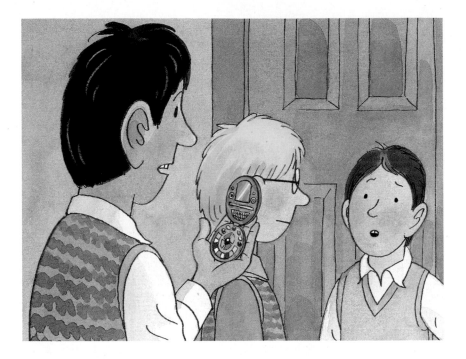

"Dunno," Tyler's voice crackled over the Link. "But listen! Get to a big house called Bletchley Park. Loads of people work there. They intercept Nazi messages in code and try to decipher them. It's very secret and hush-hush. Guards everywhere!"

"So we just walk in, do we, and zap a Viran or two?" said Nadim, grimly.

"It won't be easy," said Tyler.

A car hooted impatiently outside the school gate. "That's Mr King," said the boy. "He picks me up every day. He's on the staff at Bletchley Park. He works in the grounds. So I help him until the end of his shift."

"Ah!" said Nadim. "Nice one! I think we may have found the way to get into Bletchley Park."

Chapter 4

M r King was glad that Peter had found some friends. Peter was a shy boy who missed his mother. It was not easy for a nine-year-old to be sent away from home to live with strangers. No wonder he cried so often, and sometimes wet his bed.

"What a terrible thing the war is!" sighed Mr King. "It's a battle everyone has to fight, not just soldiers."

When they got to Bletchley Park, Mr King left the four children to play football and got on with his work.

"Don't go near the house," he warned.

Peter punted the heavy, leather football at Kipper.

"Ouch!" yelled Kipper. He had tried to head the leather football. "Don't you have a plastic ball?" he complained.

"What's plastic?" asked Peter.

Wilma was listening to her Link. "Tyler's got something," she said. "The Nazis have machines, called Enigma, that scramble messages into code before they are sent out. Then they use machines to unscramble them at the other end. Here, at Bletchley, they get hold of the coded messages. It takes weeks to break the codes even though they have copied the Enigma machines."

"But if they have the same machines here, why is it so hard?" asked Nadim.

"The Enigma machines have millions of settings," said Wilma. "The Nazis change them all the time, so the codes are never the same."

"What if they've found a way to break the codes more quickly?" said Nadim, excitedly. "If they knew the settings, they could crack the codes and see what the Nazis are up to."

"What if the Virans did something to stop it?" agreed Wilma. "Then our mission is to zap the Virans first, before it's too late. It won't be easy. Look."

They glanced across at the house. It was a large, rambling building with odd windows, archways and pointed gables. Next to it were rows of wooden huts.

A number of men and women had come out of the huts to sit on the grass in the sun.

"It's hard to spot any Virans among that
lot," said Kipper.

One woman sat away from the others.
Something about her was different.

"Hmm! Hang on," said Wilma. She ran
towards the woman, dribbling the football.

"Bet you can't tackle me," she called
loudly to the others. But as Wilma ran closer
to the woman, she took aim and kicked the
ball towards her.

The ball smacked quite hard against the woman's legs. The woman glared at Wilma with icy, blue eyes. A shadow passed over the sun. Wilma suddenly felt very cold.

"I'm ... I'm so sorry!" stuttered Wilma.

The woman stood up slowly. "Careless of you," she hissed. Then she walked off to one of the huts.

Wilma ran back to the others.

"I think I know who the Viran is," she said. "So now what are we going to do?"

"Let's wait till dark," said Nadim.

Chapter 5

"It's what we've all been hoping for,"
said the Major. "A Nazi submarine has
been captured. On board was an Enigma
machine, and a book giving us the settings."

He beamed at the others in the hut and
waved his hand at a small machine. It had
keys like a typewriter and three wheels with
letters on. Next to it was a book of settings.

"Here they are," said the Major. "Safely delivered to Bletchley Park. Now we know the settings we can crack the codes in hours."

Suddenly, he saw Miss Vinar was staring at him. To his surprise, she handed him a drink.

"A toast," she smiled. "I've been saving it for this very moment, when we had some good news like this."

It was not like the icy Miss Vinar to be friendly. "Of course," the Major gulped. "To Enigma," he cried, holding up a chipped tea cup.

Suddenly, the lights went out with a pop. The hut was thrown into darkness. A voice shouted for an emergency generator to be switched on, but nothing happened.

Candles and torches were found. As light returned to the hut the Major's heart raced.

The machine, the settings and Miss Vinar had gone.

Chapter 6

Kipper yawned. He had been crouching in a bush for what seemed like hours, waiting and watching ...

All the huts were dark, with not a chink of light coming from any door or window. Tyler had told him it was because of the wartime blackout.

Until then, the moon had cast a silvery light on the huts. But suddenly, the moon vanished and an inky blackness came down, as if a giant hand had covered the moon.

Kipper heard someone in the hut shouting about a power cut. Then he saw a figure creep out and away into the darkness.

He spoke urgently into his Link. "Wilma! Nadim! It's her! The Viran! Coming your way. She's carrying something."

Miss Vinar had only minutes to get away. Her plan was simple. In the darkness she just had to run to the fence where she had cut a hole the night before. Then, it was only a short dash to the railway line.

She would place the Enigma machine on the track to be smashed under a train. She would jump on the same train to get away. Then her work would be done. She had also taken the book of settings. Stealing them from the code breakers at Bletchley would unravel history. Britain would lose the War.

But what she had not expected was that two children – Nadim and Wilma – would jump into her path. One of them raised an arm as if to throw something at her.

In her surprise, she dropped the heavy Enigma machine and leapt sideways, past the children, into the darkness.

"I couldn't zap her," shouted Wilma.

As the moon came out, they saw the Viran running. "She's getting away," Nadim yelled as they raced after her.

"She slipped through the fence," panted Wilma. "Quickly! We must get closer or the Zaptrap might miss."

The whistle of a train sounded. The Viran was thinking fast. She decided to jump on the train from the bridge. As long as she had

the book, her plan would succeed.

But suddenly, in the moonlight ahead of her, was a small figure. It was Peter.

Wilma gasped. What was he doing?

Peter ran towards the Viran with his arms out. The Viran stumbled, and pushed him aside, but she had been slowed down.

"Peter, run!" shouted Nadim, as he threw his Zaptrap.

The Zaptrap clicked open. It flew towards the Viran like an angry insect. The Viran burst into a shower of sparks as the Zaptrap sucked in the dark energy that once had been Miss Vinar. Peter did not see it. He was sobbing in Wilma's arms.

"I thought that woman was Mummy," sobbed Peter. Wilma held him tightly as Nadim picked up the Zaptrap and the book of settings that the Viran had dropped.

Moments later, Mr King ran up. "Peter," he gasped. "Why did you run off like that?"

35

Mr King said that Peter's mother had phoned to say she was coming to see him. They had gone to meet her, but she was not on the train. That was when Peter ran off.

Peter's face lit up when Mr King told him his mother had missed her train, but would be on the next one.

Nadim handed Mr King the book of settings. "Give these to Bletchley Park."

Kipper asked Tyler to get the portal ready.

"Mission successful," he said.

"Who are you?" asked Mr King.

But the three of them had vanished.

Tyler's Mission Report

Location:	Date:
Bletchley Park	May 1941
Mission Status:	Viran Status:
Viran plot foiled.	Zapped!

Notes:

World War 2 must have been a scary time if you were a child. It's hard to imagine it! People were worried that children who lived in cities or towns would be in danger from bombing raids, so huge numbers of children were evacuated. That meant if there was any risk of being bombed, you were sent to live in the country with complete strangers. Children had labels tied to them, as if they were parcels. Then they went by train to towns and villages, not knowing who they would be living with or if they would be split from their brothers and sisters. Imagine Biff, Chip and Kipper being split up. They'd have hated it! And what would Floppy have done?

Sign off: ....Tyler.........................

History: downloaded!
The Code Breakers

An Enigma machine

Once World War 2 began, German U-boats attacked ships bringing food and goods to Britain by sea. A U-boat would search for the food ships. When it found them, it called up other U-boats and they all attacked together to sink the ships. This meant that it was very hard for Britain to get enough food. Britain almost lost the war because of this.

MINISTRY OF FOOD

RATION BOOK

OFFICIAL PAID

HOLDER'S NAME AND REGISTERED ADDRESS

Compare with your Identity Card and report any difference to your Food Office
DO NOT ALTER

Surname
Other Names
Address

ISSUED
JULY 1942

if found return to

GREENWICH

FOOD OFF

Shopping during World War 2

The U-boats used Enigma machines to send messages to each other in code. Britain had to crack the code to beat the U-boats.

A secret base was set up at Bletchley Park. People worked night and day to break the U-boats' codes. They cracked the codes, but it took hundreds of hours. The problem was, the settings on the Enigma machines were always being changed, so the codes changed too. At last, in May 1941, a book was captured showing all the Enigma settings. After that, the code breakers at Bletchley were able to decipher the messages and warn the food ships about U-boat attacks.

For more information, see the Time Chronicles website:
www.oxfordprimary.co.uk/timechronicles

Glossary

codes *(page 6)* Codes are used to send secret messages. The message is replaced by other words, numbers or letters. *"... I enjoy solving codes."*

decipher *(page 16)* To work out the meaning of something that is written in code. *"They intercept Nazi messages in code and try to decipher them."*

evacuated *(page 14)* Sent away from danger. An evacuee is the person who is sent away. *... he had been evacuated in June 1940 with all the children at his school.*

generator *(page 27)* An engine which makes electricity. *A voice shouted for an emergency generator ...*

intercept *(page 16)* To get hold of something or someone as it goes from one place to another. *"They intercept Nazi messages in code and try to decipher them."*

Nazi *(page 16)* The political party that ruled Germany at the time of World War 2.

Official Secrets Act *(page 8)* Anybody who works with information about the safety of the country has to sign the Official Secrets Act promising to keep it secret. *"Ah! The Official Secrets Act,"* she said.

Thesaurus: Another word for ...

decipher *(page 16)* solve, interpret, fathom out, translate.

Have you read them all yet?

Level 11:

Level 12:

Time Runners

Tyler: His Story

A Jack and Three Queens

Mission Victory

The Enigma Plot

The Thief Who Stole Nothing

More great fiction from Oxford University Press:

www.winnie-the-witch.com

www.dinosaurcove.co.uk

About the Authors

Roderick Hunt MBE - creator of best-loved characters Biff, Chip, Kipper, Floppy and their friends. His first published stories were those he told his two sons at bedtime. Rod lives in Oxfordshire, in a house not unlike the house in the Magic Key adventures. In 2008, Roderick received an MBE for services to education, particularly literacy.

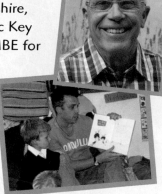

Roderick Hunt's son **David Hunt** was brought up on his father's stories and knows the world of Biff, Chip and Kipper intimately. His love of history and a good story has sparked many new ideas, resulting in the *Time Chronicles* series. David has had a successful career in the theatre, most recently working on scripts for Jude Law's *Hamlet* and *Henry V,* as well as Derek Jacobi's *Twelfth Night.*

Joint creator of the best-loved characters Biff, Chip, Kipper, Floppy and their friends, **Alex Brychta MBE** has brought each one to life with his fabulous illustrations, which are known and loved in many schools today. Following the Russian occupation of Czechoslovakia, Alex Brychta moved with his family from Prague to London. He studied graphic design and animation, before going to work on animation for Sesame Street. Since then he has devoted many years of his career to *Oxford Reading Tree,* bringing detail, magic and humour to every story! In 2012 Alex received an MBE for services to children's literature.

Roderick Hunt and Alex Brychta won the prestigious Outstanding Achievement Award at the Education Resources Awards in 2009.

42

Levelling info for parents

What do the levels mean?

Read with Biff Chip & Kipper First Chapter Books have been designed by educational experts to help children develop as readers.

Each book is carefully levelled to allow children to make gradual progress and to feel confident and enjoy reading.

The Oxford Levels you will see on these books are used by teachers and are based on years of research in schools. Below is a summary of what each Oxford Level means, so that you can help your child to improve and enjoy their reading.

The books at Level 11 (Brown Book Band):

At this level, the sentence structures are becoming longer and more complex. The story plot may be more involved and there is a wider vocabulary. However, the proportion of unknown words used per paragraph/page is still carefully controlled to help build their reading stamina and allow children to read independently.

This level mostly covers characterisation through characters' actions and words rather than through description. The story may be organised in various ways, e.g. chronologically, thematically, sequentially, as relevant to the text type and subject.

The books at Level 12 (Grey Book Band):

At this level, the sentences are becoming more varied in structure and length. Though still straightforward, more inference may be required, e.g. in dialogue to work out who is speaking. Again, the story may be organised in various ways: chronologically, thematically, sequentially, etc., so that children can reflect on how the organisation helps the reader to understand the text.

The *Times Chronicles* books are also ideal for older children who feel less confident and need more practice in order to build stamina. The text is written to be age and ability appropriate, but also engaging, motivating and funny, making them a pleasure for children to read at this stage of their reading development.

OXFORD
UNIVERSITY PRESS

Great Clarendon Street, Oxford OX2 6DP

Oxford University Press is a department of the University of Oxford.
It furthers the University's objective of excellence in research, scholarship,
and education by publishing worldwide in

Oxford New York

Auckland Cape Town Dar es Salaam Hong Kong Karachi
Kuala Lumpur Madrid Melbourne Mexico City Nairobi
New Delhi Shanghai Taipei Toronto

With offices in

Argentina Austria Brazil Chile Czech Republic France Greece
Guatemala Hungary Italy Japan Poland Portugal Singapore
South Korea Switzerland Thailand Turkey Ukraine Vietnam

Oxford is a registered trade mark of Oxford University Press
in the UK and in certain other countries

Text © Roderick Hunt

Illustrations © Alex Brychta

The moral rights of the author have been asserted

Database right Oxford University Press (maker)

First published 2010

This edition published 2016

British Library Cataloguing in Publication Data

Data available

ISBN: 978-0-19-273915-5

10 9 8 7 6 5 4 3 2 1

Illustrations by Alex Brychta

Printed in China

Paper used in the production of this book is a natural, recyclable product
made from wood grown in sustainable forests. The manufacturing process
conforms to the environmental regulations of the country of origin.

Acknowledgements: The publisher and authors would like to thank the following for their permission to
reproduce photographs and other copyright material:

P3 Iguasu/Shutterstock; P3ml Leigh Prather/Shutterstock; P4tl Blaz Kure/Shutterstock; P4tr Ragnarock/
Shutterstock; P4ml SSPL/Getty; P37 Ragnarock/Shutterstock; P38 Valentin Agapov; P38tl TSR/Shutterstock;
P38ml SSPL/Getty; P38bl Mary Evans Picture Library; P38br Mary Evans/Classic Stock/C.P. Cushing; P39tl
Popperfoto/Getty; P39bl Jose Ignacio Soto/Shutterstock; P39br SSPL/Getty; P38-39 Blaz Kure/Shutterstock;
P38-39 Jakub Krechowicz; P38-39 Picsfive/Shutterstock; P40 Blaz Kure/Shutterstock.

Book quiz answers

1 b

2 Vinar is an anagram of Viran.

3 Children who were moved from the city to the countryside during World War 2 because of the bombings.